# Old BAILLIESTON, GARROWHILL and EA

*by*
Rhona Wilson

Crosshill, behind Safeway's supermarket. Baillieston's origins stem from the population explosion of the Monklands' mining boom. Baillieston village didn't exist when Forrest's Map was drawn up in 1816 although Baillieston House did. At that time the main settlement in the area was known as Crosshill, the name (along with its religious connotations) deriving from the district's ancient landlords, the Monks of Newbattle. By 1840 maps referred to Baillieston and Crosshill as two separate places, Baillieston eventually outgrowing its parent in both size and importance. When it began to develop in the nineteenth century it was, according to the writer of the Second Statistical Account, just one of the many villages 'springing up every month'. It's likely that the village took its name from Baillieston House, possibly the seat of the Baillies of Provan who had another Baillieston estate in Dalserf parish.

# FOREWORD

Baillieston was one of countless small mining villages which developed without precedent in the early nineteenth century. The Monks of Newbattle were the first to discover and put to use the Monklands' rich deposits of 'black gold', but developing a proper coal industry was not possible until a modern transport system arrived. Miners may have been able to extract the shallow reserves easily enough; getting them to the Glasgow market was another matter. When the Monkland Canal made that possible, changes to the district's landscape, population, and whole way of life were dramatic. The writer of the Second Statistical Account reflects the confusion felt by many at the time; of Baillieston he describes a district where new villages were appearing daily and the population was increasing 'at an amazing rate'. Relying solely on coal and iron production, the Monklands' heavy industry eventually ran its course, but new schemes and villages continued to be built. Mount Vernon, Garrowhill and Easterhouse all appeared in this way but are dramatically different from each other. Despite sharing part of the Monklands' coal lands, all these areas display a highly individual character.

© Stenlake Publishing, 1997
First published in the United Kingdom, 1997
reprinted 2004, 2007, 2011
by Stenlake Publishing Limited
01290 551122
www.stenlake.co.uk

ISBN 9781840330137

Baillieston's Parish Church, known as Crosshill Church, was originally built on Crosshill Farm in the early 1830s. Previously, the only church in the Monklands was Old Monklands Parish Church at Glenmavis village (near Airdrie) which meant a long walk on Sundays. Crosshill villagers got round this by worshipping in a hall until funds were raised for a Chapel of Ease. This was eventually granted parish church status in 1783, the first chapel in Scotland to be elevated under the Church Extension scheme. By the 1960s the old church had become too small following the incorporation of Rhinsdale Church's congregation after their church was demolished. Fund-raising began again for new accommodation and St Andrews Church was built nearby. The old church is still standing, although it is somewhat the worse for wear.

GLASGOW ROAD

Before mining developed them, the tiny hamlets of Swinton, Easterhouse and West Maryston were supported by handloom weaving. Monklands was famed for its flax (which locals wove into linen) until raw cotton became widely available from America in the 1790s. Powerloom weaving also took off at this time and was, initially, rather good for the handloom weavers. At first, when the machinery was unsophisticated, it produced only yarn. This left a great surplus of thread and the handloomers were employed to make it up into material. Later, when powerlooms could also weave, the handloom industry slowly died out. Those who remained in the trade made a living out of intricate piece-work which the machines couldn't match, but by the late nineteenth century there were only a few left in Baillieston – Gavin Roy, the last one, dying in 1893.

GLASGOW ROAD

Asides from weaving the only other industry in Baillieston district before the nineteenth century was agriculture. Farms in the district were run on an open rig system with the land rented out in strips. In the long term this primitive form of farming was good neither for the farmer nor the land. A farmer wouldn't necessarily get the same rigs year after year so there was little incentive to develop or improve his patch beyond the coming season. Baillieston also seemed to have land that was in particular need of improvement – that much of it was coarse moorland was reflected in names such as Rhindmuir and Muirside. By the early 1800s the profits obtainable by selling produce at the nearby Glasgow market had been discovered and drainage, lime and manure were all beginning to be used to improve soil fertility. The old rig system died out and farms were managed in much wider areas enclosed by hedging. Heavy industry soon took precedence, however, and by the 1950s there were few farms left in Baillieston, many of them having been developed as housing schemes.

The very first miners in the Monklands were the Monks of Newbattle who, from the thirteenth century, sunk shallow bell pits and mined as much as they could before moving on to the next one. Baillieston didn't develop a proper mining industry until much later and this was only made possible when cargo transport in the form of the canal, and later the railways, opened up the mineral resources that had lain dormant for centuries. In 1790 pits were opened at Cuilhill almost simultaneously with the opening of the Monklands Canal and within a few years there was a settlement of over seventy miners at Barrachnie. The Buchanans of Mount Vernon sold mining rights on their estate as did the Bairds of Gartsherrie, the latter family becoming the district's main employers for a period of seventy-five years. Less than a century later there were pits scattered over the whole district — about thirty in all — and more being sunk.

The mining industry was helped along by development in other areas such as the iron and steel industries which needed large quantities of coal. One pit that opened in Easterhouse in the 1840s was famed for its industrial splint coal, a type of coal which was very hard and didn't clog up blast furnaces. Nearby iron and steel works which could take advantage of this included Summerlee, Calder Iron Works, Carnbroe and Langloan. Technical advances also appeared in the early nineteenth century which allowed collieries to increase their output. For instance, the Barrachnie pits which opened in 1804 were the first in Scotland to use the (fairly) new steam engine for winding coal to the surface of the pit. The effect on the district of all these developments was phenomenal as incomers came to take advantage of the new source of employment. Over the sixty years from 1831 to 1891 the population increased three-fold to around 3,600.

**BAILLIESTON CROSS**

The village's miners were a mixed bunch. Many were Irish immigrants trying to escape the recession and famines at home; others were just unemployed local weavers who still lived in their weavers' cottages. The rapid population rise led to poor conditions and there were outbreaks of disease in the cramped rows due to poor sanitation. During the 1800s there were three devastating outbreaks of cholera. Conditions were just as bad in the workplace. Baillieston's pits were difficult to work and vulnerable to dangerous flooding. Wages were low (subject as they were to the fluctuations of the market price for coal) and families survived on very basic staples such as soup, potatoes, sour milk, bread and porridge.

*Main Street, Baillieston. (East End.)* Having a holiday in this district. Was sorry you did not call before you left Portobello. How do you like Ratho? This is not such a pretty place as East Linton. L. Dewar

In 1894 Baillieston's miners went on strike for twelve weeks, along with thousands of others around the country, but this was just a taster of the hardships to come during the National Strike of 1926 which lasted about a year. During the First World War pay for miners was stable and conditions kept reasonable since their labour contributed to the war effort. Afterwards, when the industry was returned to the control of businessmen, miners were expected to accept a return to the variable wages of old. Unfortunately, although wages dropped when the going rate for coal did, they were less likely to rise when the price was good. Uncles' pawn shop in Baillieston was much frequented in the twenties and thirties by women pawning their husband's Sunday suit for a week to pay for food until pay day.

MAIN STREET LOOKING EAST, BAILLIESTON. A.5424.

For recreation, miners could choose from the usual pursuits of quoiting (throwing iron rings at a stick), pigeon-racing, playing in the band or going to dances. A more violent species of pastime, however, seemed to reflect the tension and danger of their daily lives. Blood sports, in the form of cock-fighting, dog-fighting or just man-to-man, were as popular in Baillieston as they were in mining communities elsewhere. Cock-fights, which could last anything from a few minutes to quarter of an hour, attracted holiday crowds at Provan Hall. Some were serious gamblers while others came just for the spectacle of two animals killing or maiming each other. It was considered more humane to put steel spurs over the cocks' natural ones because the kill was quicker. When sports of this type were banned as barbaric, they simply went underground. Isolated spots such as the old railway cutting at Swinton Pit and the bings at the old Camp Pit were used for illegal fights, and even today the occasional case crops up in the papers.

MAIN STREET, BAILLIESTON.

In the early years of the twentieth century there were only two other sizeable industries in Baillieston district asides from mining: the large sweetie factory and Findlay's nurseries off the Edinburgh Road. With such meagre resources it's hardly surprising the village went into a recession when the pits started to close. There were various reasons for the mines winding down. Some of the pits were simply worked out after a century of intense mining, while others, despite coal still remaining, were uneconomic to mine. Baillieston's perennial flooding problem didn't help either and there were fears that some mines were unsafe. Even before the National Strike local miners had started to leave for areas which still had large, workable pits such as Ayrshire, the Lothians and Fife. Others took their chances further afield – editions of the Airdrie and Coatbridge Advertiser from the twenties and thirties feature ads describing opportunities in Canada, New Zealand and so on.

By the late 1930s the population decrease was beginning show up in various ways. The roll of Swinton Primary dropped by almost fifty per cent to 156 pupils as families moved away from Swinton and Easterhouse to find work. Soon after the Second World War almost every pit had closed, Calderbank Pit believed to have been the last in the vicinity to go. Baillieston's Miners' Welfare, built with unfortunate timing just as the industry was waning in 1924, had to carve out a new career as a public hall.

As Baillieston's population increased throughout the nineteenth century, local services developed. The village's first police station and gas works both appeared in 1863. At this point coal was cheap enough for a group of villagers to set up the gas works privately, raising funds by selling shares at a pound each. Street lighting was eventually introduced in 1880 by persuading some public-spirited individuals to help pay for it – six street lamps in Main Street were funded this way. The police station lasted until 1948 when it was replaced by a quaint new building on Main Street which looks out of date already. Street bookies were the cause of Keystone Kop high jinks in Baillieston's past. Taking bets in the street was of course illegal and a running battle went on between the bookies and the constables. Policemen would pose as punters to try and entrap the bookies, who themselves always had a couple of look-outs to deal with such impostors.

Rhinsdale United Free Church, Baillieston.

Rhinsdale Church has been demolished, the empty space now used as a billboard site. The old surrounding wall (with a space for the church entrance) is the only part of it left standing. The church was established in the 1860s, with meetings organised in a school building in Fauldshill. Subscriptions began for a building soon after and James Neilson (inventor of hot blast smelting used in iron production) donated a site. The church opened in 1864 but a century later the congregation struggled to get a full-time minister and was eventually merged with that of St Andrews in 1966.

Plans for a tramway system that would include Baillieston first appeared in the 1870s. The Glasgow & Monkland District and the Glasgow, Coatbridge & Airdrie tramways companies both put proposals forward but had them thrown out by Parliament for being too competitive. Nothing further was heard until over twenty years later. This time a scheme was approved and a private tramway company began to serve Airdrie and Coatbridge in 1904. Baillieston, however, still had to make do with its train service because at that time it lay between the routes of the two main operators. Glasgow Corporation Tramways' route to Barrachnie was eventually extended to Baillieston in 1906 and about seven years later the Corporation agreed to extend its track to Coatbridge and link up with the private company. This was delayed by the First World War so work did not begin on this plan until the early twenties.

By the twenties the popularity of trams was waning. Motor buses were much more flexible and often faster, although tram fares were usually cheaper. A gradual withdrawal of tram services began in the early fifties until in November 1956 the Baillieston to Coatbridge and Airdrie service was closed. The following month Airdrie Town Council asked Glasgow Corporation to reintroduce trams because of the Suez crisis, but to no avail. Baillieston terminus remained in use until the next year when it was moved from the private track to Martin Crescent. Tram rails were torn up and Coatbridge Road eventually converted to a dual carriageway. By March 1962 the last tram service to Baillieston (No.15) had been replaced by Corporation buses.

Main Street again, this time a little further down near the Rhinsdale Tavern. The Monklands coal reserves couldn't reach a market without an efficient transport system and in 1770 an Act of Parliament was passed authorising the construction of the Monklands Canal. Work began the same year with James Watt (inventor of the steam engine) planning the canal course and supervising its construction. Despite its numerous backers the project ran out of money as it was much more technically complicated than had first been considered. In 1789 the whole operation was put up for sale and William Stirling and Sons, who bought the lot, had to finance the rest of the job. When the canal opened in 1790 speculators began to sink pits immediately, with some positioned right at the canal banks for easy access to the transport system. Coat's Pit was so close to the canal that three of its miners died in 1796 when the canal burst its banks and flooded the mine workings.

AS415 MAIN STREET AND EDINBURGH ROAD, BAILLIESTON.

By the 1830s the coal industry had outgrown its transport system. The establishment of iron works and steel works had dramatically increased traffic on the canal and there were whispers that a railway system would be much more effective. Pits were also being sunk further afield which meant that getting the coal to the canal was a problem. The canal reacted by cutting its rates to a third of their standard charge and investing money in building new reservoirs and loading wharves but by the mid-1860s the Monklands railway network was seventy-two miles long and one of the most profitable in the country. The canal suffered correspondingly.

By the 1870s Baillieston was completely covered as far as transport was concerned, served by two railway systems as well as the canal. In that decade the North British Railway constructed a line to Coatbridge and Easterhouse via Bathgate. At the same time the Caledonian Railway established a route between Carlisle and Glasgow via Coatbridge and Baillieston, opening the station pictured here. The railways began to lose profit when the pits closed but lasted another forty years before closing down completely in 1965. There is now new housing at Station Road, which is also near the site of Baillieston Juniors Football Park. This must have led to more recent demand for rail transport as a new station has been opened off Caledonia Road.

Muirhead Road, Baillieston.

Muirhead Road was once known as Dickson's Brae. Mr Dickson was a doctor who set up in Baillieston in the 1830s and lived at Lily Bank House at the top of the road. He was believed to have been a witness for the prosecution at the infamous Madeleine Smith trial. Twenty-one year old Smith had a French lover whom she allegedly poisoned with the same kind of chemical which she had previously tried to buy from Mr Dickson. The court seemed to find the content of her love-letters, which alluded to their sex life, more shocking than the crime. More shocking still was the fact that she continued the liaison with the victim-to-be after she became engaged to another – sophisticated play indeed for a young Victorian woman. In the end, Madeleine was set free. Her claim that she bought arsenic to improve her complexion may have palled but murder was impossible to prove using the forensics of the time.

MUIRHEAD ROAD

John Wheatley, from an Irish mining family, settled in Baillieston and served as a Labour Minister of Health. Wheatley went down the pit in 1880 when he was eleven and his experiences led him to form the Catholic Socialist Society some twenty-five years later. He wrote pamphlets denouncing capitalism in the mining industry; one ploy was to write about a trial of the coalmasters, accused of stealing the profits which should rightfully go to the miners who earned them. His meetings in Glasgow attracted crowds of about 200 but this didn't impress the Catholic church. The numbers willing to denounce his activities were far higher, and on one evening 2,000 people marched to his home to burn an effigy of him on his doorstep. Ironically, Wheatley's interest in the working class cause led him to a lifestyle far removed from his origins; his cabinet position managed to afford him Braehead House in Tollcross as a residence.

Baillieston Faulds (Scots for a livestock pen) is still recognisable today, despite the new housing. Edinburgh Road runs across the front of this picture with Faulds Gardens leading off further up on the right.

New Houses, Baillieston.

Lanarkshire County Council built steadily throughout the 1920s and 30s. Despite this there was still a housing shortage (as there was across the country) with up to three families sharing some homes. At that time it was considered unusual for newly married couples to be able to move into their own place – many had to make do with bunking up with the in-laws until their circumstances improved. By 1939 the population of Baillieston and the surrounding districts was 6,000, although the recently built Garrowhill was catching up at 4,000.

PUBLIC PARK, BAILLIESTON.

The provision of education in Scotland was severely lacking until the mid-seventeenth century. At that point an Act of Parliament was passed making landlords responsible for providing a school in every parish, which didn't achieve much because most of them ignored it. Later, education became a church responsibility and parish schools with reasonable standards gradually appeared. The system became more professional when the 1872 Education Act placed control in the hands of School Boards, elected by ratepayers. Old Monklands School Board in Baillieston took over the running of three private and four sessional (church) schools.

Baillieston House stood between Baillieston and Barrachnie, behind where Bannerman High is today. Built some time in the 1600s, it was owned by the Maxwell family throughout its long life. The Maxwell lands included Baillieston, Barrachnie and Garrowhill. Baillieston estate was taken over for building by Lanarkshire County Council and the mansion house was unoccupied for several years. Eventually it was vandalised and burned down and its remains were demolished in 1964.

Calderbank House, Baillieston.

The entrance to Calderbank House is at the foot of Hangman's Brae. A coalmaster, Mr Young, was its occupier through the late nineteenth to early twentieth century. Having lain empty for a time it became another of Lanarkshire County Council's country house acquisitions and was converted into a maternity hospital (a sub-division of Bellshill Maternity Hospital). By 1975 the house had been taken over by Glasgow District Council but was once again unoccupied. Today it is used as a refuge for alcoholics, run by the Talbot Association.

Rhinsdale House was situated near the site of the Little Chef restaurant on Edinburgh Road. Before the A8 was opened the section of Edinburgh Road from the entrance to the traffic lights at Baillieston formed part of the estate's policies. One of Rhinsdale's occupiers was Mr Webster, a Glasgow cattle dealer, who was also the last person to live at Calderpark House before that estate was converted into a zoo.

Loancroft House was the residence of Dr Willis whose father (also a doctor) moved to Baillieston in the mid-1800s. Dr Willis carried on his father's practice after his death in the late 1870s until the start of the First World War. Doctors were sorely needed in Baillieston over the course of the nineteenth century. As well as being on call to deal with industrial accidents at the pits there were several cholera epidemics caused by poor sanitation in the overcrowded properties. The 1879 outbreak was so severe that joiners in the village were conscripted as coffin makers. Bodies were buried under tar in Crosshill Churchyard on land bought for the purpose by the Department of Health. Dr Willis did his rounds on horseback and was known for his kindness – apparently he allowed pit ponies to graze on his land. Loancroft became a residential home for the elderly and was eventually replaced by a modern building in 1951. Its pillared entrance remains, however, marking the site of the old mansion house.

Baillieston's first Roman Catholic family came to the district around the mid-nineteenth century. They settled at Barrachnie and apparently had to contend with local resentment. Nevertheless, more families settled and for the next couple of decades had to walk miles to worship on a Sunday, firstly into Glasgow and, later, to a church in Coatbridge. In the early 1870s St Bridget's current site was bought and a stable on the grounds converted into a school. The church was built in 1893.

Episcopal Church, Baillieston.

St John's Episcopal Church was known as the English Kirk. Opening in the mid-nineteenth century, the building was paid for by donations from both incoming miners and the coal masters, who were keen to finance facilities such as churches, public halls or bowling greens because they felt they had a sobering influence on their workforce. St John's had particularly good relations with the Roman Catholic St Bridget's Church nearby, and when an Episcopal bishop threatened to close the English Kirk because of its falling membership, St Bridget's priest arranged for his flock to join the Episcopalians in their church on the day the bishop came to inspect it. The Bishop was suitably impressed by the numbers, and the church was saved.

Swinton Village, Baillieston

Swinton was a weaving village long before the name of Baillieston was ever introduced to the district. It also has far more ancient roots. In 1936 farm workers, filling in an old railway cutting that led to Swinton Pit, uncovered old pots thought to date back to the Bronze Age.

Swinton Crescent, Baillieston.

The houses in Swinton Crescent were built during the inter-war years as part of the 'Homes for Heroes' scheme. A hero of the Second World War, Baillieston man William Reid earned the VC for a night-raid on Hamburg which went horribly wrong. With his navigator dead, the plane damaged and himself injured he still managed to reach his target, successfully bomb it and return home. Unfortunately, on a later mission he had to bale out of his bomber and spent the rest of the war as a POW in Germany.

Swinton Primary on Rhindmuir Road was built because of overcrowding at Baillieston School and opened on 27 August 1929. It also accommodated pupils from the small schoolhouse at Easterhouse at a time when much of the population of West Maryston was being resettled in Baillieston. Despite this big intake the numbers dropped over the years and there were just 100 pupils on the school roll and only part of the building in use in the 1950s.

Bargeddie existed long before its larger neighbour, Baillieston. In Pont's Map of 1596 it appears as Balgedy, almost two centuries before a map reference to Baillieston House appears. Bargeddie School was built as a venue for both teaching and worship at a time when the community couldn't afford two separate buildings. Later, when it wasn't needed for either, it was sold to a railway company which resulted in a fierce dispute in the courts over whether the school board or the church owned it. The church won a settlement which gave it enough money to build a hall.

Bargeddie was reasonably well served by public transport in the early twentieth century. In 1923 Glasgow Corporation extended its tramways through the village to Coatbridge on the 2½ mile long private tram-line pictured here. Bargeddie Railway Station first opened as Cuilhill before it was renamed in 1904. Passenger services from there were relatively short-lived as it closed temporarily during the First World War and then for good in 1927. Thereafter the station was used for freight transport alone (until closure in the sixties) and locals relied on the burgeoning bus services of Scottish General Transport, Midland Bus Service and then SMT.

This 1910 picture of Mount Vernon in its sparse setting gives some indication of how the district earned its original name. Until the late eighteenth century it was known as Windy Edge, easily explained by a short visit to the unsheltered, rather bleak estate. In 1756 the lands were acquired by the Glasgow tobacco merchant, George Buchanan, who favoured a more flattering name. Both he and his brother in Virginia changed their estates' names at the same time in honour of the popular British Admiral Vernon. These days Mount Vernon is kept in its place by less well off neighbours who label it Spam Valley. This, a kind of 'all fur coat and no knickers' damnation, implies that its inhabitants spend so much money on their homes they must surely make do with spam for the dinner table.

BOWLING GREEN. MOUNT VERNON.
538

Although Mount Vernon was his country residence, George Buchanan also built Virginia Mansions on the outer edges of Glasgow. Acquiring estates such as these was fairly common amongst nouveau riche tobacco lords, who mostly obtained them with hard cash as opposed to the traditional route of inheritance. It was a sound investment for several reasons. Firstly, it gave them and their descendants social distinction and access to local politics. Landowners were a class apart and also much involved in local decision-making such as the selection of ministers and teachers. In addition, it was also an asset which could be rented out to farmers or mortgaged to raise a loan. By the late eighteenth century land itself had become a resource with estates in the mineral rich Monklands being sought after by entrepreneurial merchants. Many who had invested in the Monklands Canal made further canny investments in the surrounding areas which would be developed into coal fields.

When George Buchanan died at just thirty-four, his family chose to keep the estate on for some years, as they did their Drumpellier and Corsewell estates. Lieutenant Colonel David Carrick Buchanan was the last family occupier, living at Mount Vernon until the late nineteenth century. From the 1860s onwards he sold bits of the estate off for building. The first person to buy in Mount Vernon was Fyffe Christie, the Glasgow writer, who bought a plot for building large villas near Hamilton Road. This initial speculator seems to have set the style for the development of the estate as a whole. Over the years many other builders did the same and Mount Vernon is now full of homes for the wealthy which seem to hark back to a different era.

Garrowhill House was situated at the top of what is now Garrowhill Park and was owned by J.M. Scott Maxwell of the Baillieston Estate. Maxwell sold off Garrowhill in the 1930s for development as a private housing estate, which he also believed would be an important social experiment. After the First World War British society was in the grip of change. Reports of the time are full of references as to how the old customs were dying out and the working classes, worn down by unemployment and poverty, underwent a political transformation expressed in the national strikes of the time. The establishment was clearly threatened and Maxwell hoped that building well-designed homes with full amenities, such as at Garrowhill, would create happy communities, contented with the political status quo. He believed that 'when there [were] thousands of such communities throughout the land the effect on the country [would be] to counteract the spread of Communism and Fascism'.

THE BOWLING GREEN, GARROWHILL.    A.5422.

With his grandiose plan, Maxwell is a difficult man to judge. He seemed aware of the harshness of working class life and the insanity of throwing up post-war housing with little thought to an infrastructure to support it. His desire for people to have a decent education (a school was a central part of the scheme) and broaden their horizons culturally seem genuine enough. Nevertheless 'Garrowhill' was a commercial proposition and Maxwell's easy philanthropy and academic interest in 'ordinary people' smacks of the all too familiar paternalism of the upper classes. One telling remark of his relays his indignation at 'someone who couldn't co-operate with his neighbour' criticising the prime minister. He considered this 'a travesty of democracy' and in this light his interest in Garrowhill seems more an expression of his own fears and inability to cope with a changing world; an attempt to halt the development of an alien society where the establishment could be questioned.

*This is a picture of our new house. We are only paying 15/11ᵈ a week including Rates & Taxes.*

Building began at Garrowhill in 1934 and over 13,000 houses had been completed when work was interrupted by the start of the Second World War. This postcard was produced to advertise the development and features a printed 'hand-written' message on the back written by 'Grace' and expressing her satisfaction with her new home: 'What a delightful change it is to live in a really well designed house. You remember that awful time we had in our last flat with the wireless fiend who lived above us?' She goes on to provide helpful directions, 'PS Take an Airdrie bus from Buchanan Street and ask the conductor to let you off at Garrowhill Estate'. Garrowhill offered spacious homes, shops, churches, schools, and advertised a better class of neighbour.

Barrachnie shops, Garrowhill. Barrachnie village suffered fluctuating fortunes throughout the centuries. In 1794 the hamlet had a population of just seventy-five colliers. Some forty years later it could boast a working population of 3,000, occupied in the local coal and iron trade. The original village survived until Barrachnie Colliery closed in the mid-1930s and the area was developed as a small shopping zone for the residents of Garrowhill and Mount Vernon.

Camp Road. Garrowhill.

Camp Road was named after Camp Colliery, the position of which is marked by the roundabout on Thornbridge Road. Despite having been in existence for over sixty years Garrowhill has little strong identity of its own amidst the surrounding settlements. There is no Main Street or natural focus asides from the church and Barrachnie shops and you would hesitate to label it as a village or town in the normal sense. Today it is very much a dormitory of the comfortably-off, lived in by those who do most of their working, shopping and playing elsewhere.

SWINTON CROSS, EASTERHOUSE.

D.D. Smith, Easterhouse.

Easterhouse offers a startling contrast to Garrowhill and it may come as a surprise to some to find out that the infamous housing scheme can claim a long history. Provan Hall is still standing in Easterhouse and dates from the 1470s when it was a country seat for the prebendaries of Glasgow Cathedral, one of whom was James IV. By connection, the old village was known as 'the Holy land', one of a cluster of mining villages including West Maryston and Swinton. Easterhouse Road, pictured here, was the focal point of the village with its general stores as well as the Co-op near the railway. Vans and carts from nearby farms supplied meat and milk and Jimmy Young of the Brig Bar provided the beer. These days, what was once the village centre is now mainly a thoroughfare and most of its shops are long gone.

When rebuilding started in the inter-war years the authorities took the decision to run down Easterhouse village. At the time street lighting was being introduced and roads which didn't get this were effectively condemned. The old school, built in 1895, was vacated in 1920 in favour of a new primary at Swinton and the council bought up sites on either side of Baillieston Main Street for building new houses for the displaced population. Despite the move many people still worked in Easterhouse (at the tube or waggon works) and so continued to frequent their old pubs. The buildings in the left foreground of this picture are now gone but housed Mr Stewart's grocers and Jimmy Young's pub. A plaque on Easterhouse Road bridge commemorates Jimmy as a benefactor who gave as much money back to the community as he took in payment for beer.

MAIN ST EASTERHOUSE

D.D. Smith Easterhouse

Easterhouse as we know it today began in the 1950s. At the time Glasgow was struggling with acute housing problems following major slum clearance programmes, and to cope with demand, began building high-rise schemes on the edge of the city. The haste to build places such as Drumchapel, Castlemilk and Easterhouse is reflected in their birth-dates; 1952, 1953 and 1954 respectively. Initially, Easterhouse was a highly desirable option to families living in the cramped single-ends of the inner city. Its two bed-roomed flats were unusually spacious and the experience was promoted as 'like living in the country'. A visit to the vetting office was a big occasion because it was known that agents (who had a reputation for occasional abuse of their power of allocation) were fussy. An airing of your Sunday best was called for and people had to have an income of a certain level before even being considered.

EASTERHOUSE FROM THE SOUTH.                              D.D. Smith, Easterhouse.

Some of Easterhouse's first residents thought they were living in a country paradise, encouraged by the fact that they had to go to the local farm for eggs and milk.  But just ten years after the first intake the scheme was infamous as a gangland – one of its main problems being the lack of amenities which had made it so charming to begin with.  The authorities' mistake was that Easterhouse was a housing scheme made up of houses alone.  In the post-war haste to rebuild, it was planned without shops, churches or recreational facilities.  The proposed shopping centre at Bogbain and Shandwick Street was delayed for years because of coal seams supposedly underneath it and even when the population had reached 60,000 there was still no police station.  Those that could started to move back to the city and the scheme dropped to the bottom of the council's table of popularity for the areas on their housing list.  For those who remained a life of poverty and unemployment began.

EASTERHOUSE FROM CANAL

To begin with, the press in the 1960s seemed interested only in reporting sensationalist tales about Easterhouse's gangs instead of on the underlying social problems which were responsible for them. When cases of youth violence made the courts the scheme became internationally known. One positive outcome of the attention was that Frankie Vaughan volunteered his services in 1968 in support of a youth project set up to combat the gangs. Part of Easterhouse's problem was that it was made up of a disadvantaged and transient community with little of the healthy cross-section of society that appeared in other settlements. No lawyers or doctors lived there, for example, and hardly anybody else wanted to – one set of church statistics showed 30% of those who moved in, moved out again within a year.

CANAL WEST MARYSTON, EASTERHOUSE.   D.D. Smith, Easterhouse

These days Easterhouse is surviving due to improvements, such as the home-steading scheme of the 1980s, which encouraged people to buy flats cheaply and upgrade them. A 'right stushie' was caused when Princess Diana visited one such street – it was later discovered that the residents got £2,000 grants to make their homes even more palatable for the visit. Eventually, the district also got its shopping mall, library and swimming pool. Despite this, a common local complaint is the lack of quality shops. Chains avoid setting up in Easterhouse and the shops which are there seem to have few qualms about charging comparatively high prices to their captive market. One noticeable effect of poverty, however, is the existence of strong, local self-help initiatives, such as the credit union set up in 1990. And despite it all, you will still find people who have lived there all their lives, have no plans to move, and speak very warmly of the community indeed.